THE MIRACLE OF DEBT RELEASE

Dr. Creflo A. Dollar Jr.

Unless otherwise indicated, all Scripture quotations are taken from the *King James Version* of the Bible.

Scripture quotations marked *AMP* are taken from *The Amplified Bible, New Testament*

Copyright © 1960, 1962, 1963, 1968, 1971, 1972, 1973, 1975, 1977 by The Lockman Foundation. Used by permission.

The Miracle of Debt Release
ISBN 1-885072-25-2
Copyright © 1999 by Dr. Creflo A. Dollar Jr.

Published by:
Creflo Dollar Ministries
P.O. Box 490124
College Park, GA 30349

TABLE OF CONTENTS

INTRODUCTION

Child of God, Jesus is on His way back! I would not be at all surprised if He showed up within the not-too-distant future. Everyone is expecting Him to return in the year 2000—even sinners. But I do not believe He will come then. Why? There is a New Testament Scripture that must first be fulfilled.

2 Peter 3:3,4

Knowing this first, that there shall come in the last days scoffers, walking after their own lusts, And saying, Where is the promise of his coming? for since the fathers fell asleep, all things continue as they were from the beginning of the creation.

You see, after the day of Jesus' anticipated return has come and gone, the scoffers and unbelievers will mock us saying, "He's not going to show up." But if you don't believe anything else you read in the Bible, believe the Scriptures that confirm His inevitable return (Acts 1:11; 15:16-18). However, before you start rejoicing and planning for that glorious occasion, know that He will not be coming back for a Church that is broke, depressed, and out of His divine will!

Jesus will not come back for a Church enslaved by debt, whose finances are used to contribute to the wealth of the wicked. The Bible tells us in Ephesians 5:27 that He's coming back for a Church without spot, wrinkle, or blemish. *Debt is a wrinkle!* That means that the Body of Christ will have to be debt-free before Jesus comes back. Our finances must be used exclusively to fund the Gospel and to bless others. In other words, as a Body, we must corporately experience the miracle of debt release. We will have to renew our minds with the Word of God to see debt as He sees it. Then we can take the necessary steps to banish debt from our lives. God has made provision in His Word that we should *"owe no man any thing, but to love one another..."* (Romans 13:8), but we've got to do our part.

If you have never considered the possibility of living debt-free, let this book be the beginning to a life of freedom from the oppression of debt. If you only learn one thing from this book, learn that there is an anointing available to miraculously release you from every financial burden. Child of God, you can be free from debt in Christ Jesus; and *"if the Son therefore shall make you free, ye shall be free indeed"* (John 8:36).

DELIVERANCE FROM CAPTIVITY

Luke 4:18,19

The Spirit of the Lord is upon me, because he hath anointed me to preach the gospel to the poor; he hath sent me to heal the broken hearted, to preach deliverance to the captives, and recovering of sight to the blind, to set at liberty them that are bruised, To preach the acceptable year of the Lord.

If you think debt cancellation will happen without the anointing, think again. In this passage of Scripture, Jesus proclaims He is anointed to preach the *Gospel*—the "good news." The good news is that Jesus has the "burden-removing, yoke-destroying" power of God to handle every situation. He boldly proclaims that He is anointed to remove your burdens and destroy your yoke of debt.

When God purposed to remove the burden of debt, it was an act of the anointing. Jesus is anointed to release those in captivity. If you've ever been in debt, you know that debt is captivity. The good news is that He has an anointing to remove your debt. Now, if you're waiting to see what the government or the stock market is going to do about your debt, you're looking in the wrong places. Why? Because only

God alone has the power to miraculously cancel your debt and give you the life of freedom promised in His Word.

The power of God is where your faith should be for the answer to this and every problem you face in life. First Corinthians 2:5 says that we should have no faith *"...in the wisdom of men, but in the power of God."* God has a way to get you out of whatever financial difficulty you're in right now. If debt release is what you're after, have confidence in God's power—His Word. Begin to factor in the anointing whenever you are preparing a budget or tackling a mountain of bills. You've got to settle in your heart that there is indeed an anointing available to wipe out all of your debt!

God's anointing can remove every burden and destroy every yoke in your life. It's the same with your debt. You may think that going to the bank to borrow money is the solution, but you're simply adding to the problem. Think about it— when you borrow money you're still in debt. Instead, when you are faced with a lack of resources or finances, place a demand on the anointing of God. Speak the Word over your situation, thank God for the anointing power to get you out, and put pressure on the Word to remove your debt forever. I tell you it works!

Remember when Paul came to Jesus complaining about the thorn in his side and asked Him to remove it? Jesus responded *"...My grace is sufficient for thee: for my strength is made perfect in weakness"* (2 Corinthians 12:9). God's willingness to get involved in your affairs never changes. That same grace and anointing is as sufficient for you today as it was for Paul then. The anointing is guaranteed to deliver you from the captivity of debt. Hallelujah!

DIRECTED NOT DRIVEN

The *anointing* is defined as "the burden-removing, yoke-destroying power of God." If you neither know nor have confidence in the anointing that is on Jesus, you will continue to bear your burdens alone. You will live a life driven by your situations and circumstances rather than one directed by the Word of God. A driven life is filled with stress, worry, and fear; a Word-directed life is filled with peace.

Psalm 37:23 reads, ***"The steps of a good man are ordered by the Lord: and he delighteth in his way."*** When you allow God to order your steps, you will live in the peace of being in His perfect will. The written Word and time spent in the presence of God should serve as your reference guide for direction.

It is God's will that we prosper. Psalm 35:27 says that God takes ***"...pleasure in the prosperity of his servant."*** However, prosperity is more than money; it is freedom from debt. Getting out of debt and staying in complete control of your finances puts you in a prosperous position to be a blessing. God is pleased when you are free to do whatever He directs you to do with your finances. It brings Him great sow to advance the Gospel.

Living a directed life puts you in a position to bless others. In fact, it is God's will that we bless others. Genesis 12:3 says, ***"...and in thee shall all families of the earth be blessed."*** There is no way to meet someone else's needs if your own needs are not being met. If you are "robbing Peter to pay Paul," you are being driven into hopelessness rather than being directed into joy.

THE JOY OF THE LORD

I want to help you get to the place where you are living a life directed by the Spirit of God—the ideal place to be. As you begin the process of debt cancellation, I encourage you to maintain a spirit of joy. Remember *"...the joy of the Lord is your strength"* (Nehemiah 8:10).

The joy of the Lord is your defense against every challenge in life. The spirit of debt cannot harm you if you're walking in the joy of the Lord and the power of His Word. Don't allow yourself to become depressed in the process of debt cancellation. Keep in the forefront of your mind the fact that God's Word will do what it says it will do. You may or may not see results right away, but don't give up! Even if others around you experience manifestation before you do, stay encouraged. God is about to perform a miracle in your life. The Word says, *"Rejoice with them that do rejoice..."* (Romans 12:15). By doing so, you will set yourself up for the same miracle. Stick to the Word. It works!

THE STEPS OF A
RIGHTEOUS MAN

Some Christians stay in the same predicament even after hearing anointed teachings that have the power to change their lives. Decide now that you will not be one of them. Failing to execute what you learn produces empty results.

Here are six steps to get you out of debt. They involve discipline, determination, and diligence. This is an anointed plan of action for your miracle of debt release.

1. Create a list of every bill you owe.

Knowing exactly how much you owe is vital. God is a God of divine order and details. Divine order is a prerequisite for miracles. Jesus had the multitude to sit in groups of fifty before miraculously feeding them with a loaf of bread and two pieces of fish (Luke 9:14-17). Therefore, it is imperative that you operate in the highest level of accountability in order to launch an effective attack against the spirit of debt. *"For which of you, intending to build a tower, sitteth not down first, and counteth the cost, whether he have sufficient to finish it?"* (Luke 14:28).

2. Ask God for the specific financial miracle you need.

Begin to speak to your mountain of debt. Do this by reciting aloud the name of each creditor and the exact balance owed. Use the Word of God to make your confession and expect God to cancel every one, down to the penny. Matthew 17:20 says, *"...If ye have faith as a grain of mustard seed, ye shall say unto this mountain, Remove hence to yonder place; and it shall remove; and nothing shall be impossible unto you."*

3. Thank God for progress in reducing your debt.

Your first financial miracle may be small, but acknowledge that it came from God, and realize that more is on the way. When you do this, God will multiply His favor in your life. God wants you to worship Him and trust Him as your source for everything that you desire in life, including debt freedom. When you acknowledge what He does on your behalf, He is moved to do even more. God appreciates thankfulness. If you don't acknowledge financial miracles, they will cease. Your faith in God will produce the desired result. *"Now faith is the substance of things hoped for, the evidence of things not seen"* (Hebrews 11:1).

4. Become a tither in a good, local church.

How do you define *good*? If the Word of God is being taught with knowledge and understanding and the ministry is faithful to do what God instructs it to do, it is a good church and good ground for sowing your seed.

Malachi 3:10

Bring ye all the tithes into the storehouse, that there may be meat in mine house, and prove me now herewith, saith the Lord of hosts, if I will not open you the windows of heaven, and pour you out a blessing, that there shall not be room enough to receive it.

Be sure to tithe. God only requires that you give ten percent of your earnings to be used as seed to help manage His house—the church. The tithe is your covenant connector. It keeps the windows of heaven open over your life. Your debt can't be cancelled if the windows of heaven are closed. God promises an abundant return on the tithe—more than you can contain.

14

5. Become a partner with ministries that are good ground for sowing.

This relationship is necessary because you will need additional ground in which to sow your offering. Your tithe opens the windows of heaven while your offering determines the amount of your harvest. Your offering enables God to pour out financial blessings in your life.

Luke 6:38

Give, and it shall be given unto you; good measure, pressed down, and shaken together, and running over, shall men give into your bosom. For with the same measure that ye mete withal it shall be measured to you again.

If you give, it will be given to you. It's that simple. You can go crying to God, "Lord I need you to help me," but He'll just say, "I need you to help me, too—give!" Create an out-of-debt flow. Money out means money in. Plant a seed and reap the harvest. This is the process of seedtime and harvest (Genesis 8:22).

6. Bind the strong man.

The spirit of debt comes from the strong man, Satan, who must be tied up so that you can take back what's rightfully yours. **Mark 3:27** says, *"No man can enter into a strong man's house, and spoil his goods, except he will first bind the strong man; and then he will spoil his house."*

The Word of God declares that the strong man must return what he has stolen seven-fold (Proverbs 6:31). Announce to Satan that he will no longer be allowed to operate in your finances. Do this as often as necessary. The name of Jesus is stronger than the spirit of debt. The book of Philippians says at the name of Jesus every knee shall bow. This includes Satan and your debt, because *"...greater is He that is in you, than he that is in the world"* (1 John 4:4).

ANGELS TO THE RESCUE

Angels play a major role in your debt release. God wants you out of debt so much that He has assigned angels to help carry out the assignment of gaining your financial freedom. They are your assigned servants. *"Are not the angels all ministering spirits (servants) sent out in the service [of God for the assistance] of those who are to inherit salvation?"* (Hebrews 1:14, *AMP*).

Remember, Child of God, your mouth and your life are linked together in this process. Don't think for one moment that you will experience debt release by keeping your mouth closed. Speak to the oppressive spirit of debt. The Word says, *"...out of the abundance of the heart the mouth speaketh"* (Matthew 12:34). Command all mountains of debt to be destroyed. You can then expect the angels to hearken to the voice of the Word of God.

Psalm 103:20,21

> *Bless the Lord, ye his angels, that excel in strength, that do his commandments, hearkening unto the voice of his word. Bless ye the Lord, all ye his hosts; ye ministers of his, that do his pleasure.*

Angels do what pleases God. They are involved in your prosperity. Say continuously, *"I'm out of debt!"* Confess that it is God's will for you to be debt free. Stir yourself up by recalling examples in the Bible where people were delivered from debt: the man with the ax head (2 Kings 6:5), the woman with the cruse of oil (1 Kings 17:1-15), Nehemiah's workmen (Nehemiah 5:1-19), and David's father (1 Samuel 17:25-58).

Angels are commanded by God to hearken to the voice of His Word. I said the *voice* of *His* Word! That means you have to get involved by opening your mouth and speaking the Word, and not your own words. Angels are then obligated to work on your behalf. They can work for you everyday to bring you out of debt. When you speak the Word, you employ all of heaven just by opening your mouth! You employ Jesus, the Holy Spirit, and the angels to bring you to a point of debt release. That's why it is so vital that you pray the Word daily.

Picture the angels tiptoeing around at the credit card companies or at the IRS, engaged in activities that only God Almighty can see. He has angels working for Him, who are, in turn, working for you. The Bible says they have been sent to minister to the *"...heirs of salvation"* (Hebrews 1:14). If you are born again, you are an heir of salvation. Just keep the Word in your mouth and give voice to it, and the angels will bring in your harvest.

HE WILL HEAR AND HELP

2 Chronicles 20:9

If, when evil cometh upon us, as the sword, judgment, or pestilence, or famine, we stand before this house, and in thy presence, (for thy name is in this house,) and cry unto thee in our affliction, then thou wilt hear and help.

An *affliction* is "any problem or condition that produces suffering, loss, pain, or grief." If you've ever been entangled in the stronghold of debt, you have experienced affliction. No matter what you face, God is *"...a very present help in trouble"* (Psalm 46:1). As a child of the King, you have the opportunity to be heard and helped by your Father in heaven. Psalm 34:17 says, *"The righteous cry, and the Lord heareth, and delivereth them out of all their troubles."* When was the last time you cried to the Lord concerning your debt? Know for certain that when you do, He will hear and help.

When you are held captive by debt, there are things in the spiritual realm that are locked up and unable to work on your behalf. In order to release them, use the force of praise.

Although the fig tree shall not blossom, neither shall fruit be in the vines; the labour of the olive shall fail, and the fields shall yield no meat; the flock shall be cut off from the fold, and there shall be no herd in the stalls: Yet I will rejoice in the Lord, I will joy in the God of my salvation. The Lord God is my strength, and he will make my feet like hinds' feet, and he will make me to walk upon mine high places...

I encourage you to praise God until He unlocks in the spirit realm whatever is hindering your debt cancellation. You may not be able to figure out how you're going to get out of debt, but take the time to praise God anyway. Learn how to take authority over the spirit of debt. If it appears that your debt situation is not changing, rebuke the devil and remind him that he is bound from operating in your life. Once you do this, he has no choice but to cease and desist in his maneuvers against your finances.

Matthew 11:12 says, *"...the violent take it by force."* Debt can be overcome by force. When you become intense or violent in your efforts to become debt-free, you put a demand on the Word of God to bring the manifestation. No matter what you see around you, be persistent. God will perform miraculous debt cancellation for you if you are violent in your faith. Start expecting your debt to be released and begin looking for miracles.

Let me give you another reason to get rid of your debt: there are unbelievers watching you. Unbelievers will be convinced of God's power when they see Him moving on your behalf. Imagine what would happen if they saw you completely out of debt. Hallelujah! When your manifestation comes, tell everybody! Don't keep it to yourself—something happens when you testify. Remember that old song, "I said I wasn't gonna tell nobody, but I couldn't keep it to myself." God does even more when you tell somebody what He's done. Your deliverance benefits those who hear it. In essence, your testimony gives God praise.

CONCLUSION

There are many accounts of debt cancellation throughout the Bible. In the Book of Philemon, the Apostle Paul wrote that the debt of Onesimus, the runaway slave, was supernaturally cancelled. In 1 Samuel 17:25, David's father's debt was cancelled by Saul when David defeated Goliath. And in the Book of Nehemiah, God not only delivered His people out of debt, He restored all they lost. None of these events are recorded in the Bible as miracles. But there is one thing you can be sure of, any time a debt is cancelled for a Child of God, it is done through God's intervention. That makes every debt God cancels for a Christian a miracle.

In the Book of Exodus, God miraculously delivered the nation of Israel out of debt. Imagine that—an entire nation out of debt! They were without money and consumed by the kind of poverty that comes with slavery. Believe me, the worst type of poverty one can experience is slavery. Realize that when you are in debt you are enslaved to your credit cards and bills. *"...the borrower is servant to the lender"* (Proverbs 22:7). But praise God you're on your way out!

When the people of Israel were finally delivered from over 400 years of slavery in Egypt, they were broke. But God had a plan for their restoration.

Exodus 3:21,22

And I will give this people favour in the sight of the Egyptians: and it shall come to pass, that, when ye go, ye shall not go empty: But every woman shall borrow of her neighbour, and of her that sojourneth in her house, jewels of silver, and jewels of gold, and raiment: and ye shall put them upon your sons, and upon your daughters; and ye shall spoil the Egyptians.

Exodus 12:35 says, *"And the children of Israel did according to the word of Moses; and they borrowed of the Egyptians jewels of silver, and jewels of gold, and raiment...."* You're probably wondering why God put them in a position to borrow. God didn't give the Israelites wealth to use for themselves. The fact is, He gave it to them to prove that He would take care of them.

The Word tells us that after they had done all they could do, God opened the Red Sea. He created an avenue of escape. I believe God purposely opened the sea and allowed the

Egyptians to drown, in order to cancel the debt of the Israelites.

Israel prospered because they obeyed Moses' command. Likewise, the key to receiving your miracle is believing and trusting your man of God. The Word says in 2 Chronicles 20:20 that if you trust God and believe His prophets you will prosper. *"And Moses said unto the people, Fear ye not, stand still, and see the salvation of the LORD, which he will shew to you to day: for the Egyptians whom ye have seen to day, ye shall see them again no more for ever"* (Exodus 14:13). Israel was willing to do whatever the prophet told them to do. It was their trust and obedience that led to their deliverance. He's telling you the same thing, "Stand still and watch Me deliver you."

Exodus 14:30,31

Thus the Lord saved Israel that day out of the hand of the Egyptians; and Israel saw the Egyptians dead upon the sea shore. And Israel saw that great work which the Lord did upon the Egyptians: and the people feared the Lord, and believed the Lord, and his servant Moses.

Child of God, I am convinced that if you hold on to the peace of God's Word concerning your finances, you will see victory. If you lose one battle in this process of debt cancellation, it doesn't mean that you've lost the entire war. God is faithful. If He said it, He will do it. If He promised it, He will bring it to pass. Instead of relying on *your* strength to get out of debt, use the burden-removing, yoke-destroying, power of God as the Israelites did.

It has never been God's plan for you to rely on your strength or money as your source. It has always been His intention to provide and take care of you. In order for Him to do that however, you can no longer see your paycheck as your source for living. God wants the same thing you want—prosperity for you (3 John 2). He knows your desires and He knows what you need. Decide today that you will rely on God alone to meet your needs. Your debt deliverance begins with obedience to God.

Expect the miracle of debt release to become real in your life. If you want a miracle, don't doubt God's power. The Biblical accounts mentioned in this book are designed to reinforce the fact that if God did something once, He'll do it again. The Word declares *"Jesus Christ the same yesterday, and to day, and for ever"* (Hebrews 13:8).

Debt is a spirit of the enemy. Apply pressure

to it daily until it's completely gone. God promises us that whatever we ask in the name of Jesus, He will do (John 14:14). You are entering into a new level of glory—the freedom of debt-free living in Christ!

ABOUT THE AUTHOR

Dr. Creflo A. Dollar Jr. is the pastor and founder of World Changers Church International, a non-denominational church located in College Park, Georgia.

Formerly an educational therapist, Creflo Dollar began the ministry in 1986 with eight people. He is now an international teacher and conference speaker with a congregation of over 20,000.

Dr. Dollar has been called by God to teach the gospel with simplicity and understanding. He can be seen and heard throughout the world on the *Changing Your World* broadcast via television and radio.

FIVE STEPS TO COMPLETE SALVATION

1. Recognize and admit that you are a sinner **(Psalm 51:5)**.

2. Repent of your sins **(1 John 1:9)**.

3. Confess Jesus Christ as Lord and Savior **(Romans 10:9,10)**.

   "Father, in the name of Jesus, I recognize and admit that I am a sinner. I repent of my sin and I make a 180° turn away from sin to you by changing my heart, my mind, and direction. I confess with my mouth that Jesus is Lord, and I believe in my heart that you raised Him from the dead. I invite you to come into my life Lord Jesus, and I thank you that I am saved. Amen."

4. Receive baptism by water **(Matthew 3:6)** and the baptism of the Holy Spirit with the evidence of speaking in tongues **(Acts 2:3, 4, 38; Acts 8:14-17)**.

5. Pray, read, and obey the Word of God daily **(1 John 5:3)**.

SEVEN STEPS TO RECEIVING THE BAPTISM OF THE HOLY SPIRIT

1. The Holy Spirit is a gift that was given on the day of Pentecost **(Acts 2:38)**.

2. Salvation is the only qualification necessary for receiving the Holy Spirit **(Acts 2:38)**.

3. The laying on of hands is scriptural **(Acts 8:17)**.

4. You can expect to speak in tongues when hands are laid on you **(Acts 19:6)**.

5. Disregard any fears or false teachings about receiving a counterfeit **(Luke 11:11-13)**.

6. Open your mouth as an act of faith **(Ephesians 5:18,19)**.

7. Receive the gift of speaking in tongues in an atmosphere of peace **(1 Corinthians 14:33)**.

BOOKS BY
DR. CREFLO A. DOLLAR JR.

- Answers Awaiting in the Presence of God

- How to Honor Your Man of God

- How to Trouble Your Trouble

- S.O.S. Help! My Flesh Needs Discipline

- The Anointing to Live

- The Color of Love

- The Covenant Connector

- Having Faith for Mysteries

- Jesus Is Our Jubilee

- The Miracle of Debt Release

- How to Get Out of Debt God's Way

- How to Obtain Healing

- El Shaddai: Making a Demand on God's Supply

- How to Train Up a Child Without Breaking His
  Spirit*

(*) By Taffi L. Dollar

TAPE SERIES BY
DR. CREFLO A. DOLLAR JR.

- The Ministry of the Holy Spirit - Volumes 1 & 2
- The Inheritance of Our Salvation
- Overcoming Impossibilities
- How to Tame Your Thoughts
- How to Overcome the Spirit of Lust:
  An Unquenchable Desire
- Understanding the Will of God - Volumes 1 & 2
- Understanding God's Answer to Racism,
  Separation, and Division
- Making Jubilee a Reality in Your Life
- Having Faith for Mysteries
- Prosperity Profile
- How to Receive the End of Your Faith
- The Miracle of Debt Release
- How to Get Out of Debt God's Way
- It's Time to Believe God
- The Making, Shaping and Molding of Godly Children
- Living Under God's Commanded Blessings*
- Family Matters*
- Kidz Faith Confessions*

(*) By Taffi L. Dollar

JOIN THE TAPE CLUB

By becoming a tape club member, you will receive tapes of each Sunday service monthly by choosing a monthly, quarterly, or annual payment plan.

HEAR the **UNEDITED, UNCUT, AND UNMISTAKABLY CANDID** teachings of Dr. Creflo A. Dollar Jr. as heard by the congregation at the World Dome.

EXPERIENCE the dynamic power and...

SHARE in the excitement, joy, and inspiration as the Word of God is delivered with simplicity and understanding.

IT'S JUST LIKE BEING THERE!!

CREFLO DOLLAR MINISTRIES

ARTNERSHIP HAS ITS PRIVILEGES

Become a Vision Partner

Our part is to:
• Pray daily that God's blessings be upon you.
• Study the Word and diligently seek God on your behalf.
• Minister to you monthly in a personal letter from Dr. Creflo A. Dollar Jr.
• Provide you with an official partner certificate.
• Periodically offer special gifts for your spiritual edification and growth.

Your part is to:
• Pray for us always.
• Be committed to support meetings in your area.
• Support us financially with your monthly pledge (Phil. 4:17).
• Always lift up the ministry, Dr. Dollar, and his family with positive confessions.

If you would like:

• To order books and tapes by Dr. Creflo A. Dollar Jr.
• To become a partner or supporter of Creflo Dollar Ministries
• To obtain a free copy of the *Changing Your World* magazine

Call us:

United States and Canada 1-866-477-7683

United Kingdom ....+44-121-359-5050

Australia ....+61-7-5528-1144

South Africa ....+27-11-792-5562

Visit our web site: www.worldchangers.org

Dr. Creflo A. Dollar Jr.

The Miracle

...your debt has been cancelled

# of Debt Release